.le.

D1329368

c2004.   2-04

Who Needs Teeth?

by Janelle Cherrington

Reading Consultant: Wiley Blevins, M.A.
Phonics

Compass Point Books
3109 West 50th Street, #115
Minneapolis, MN 55410

Visit Compass Point Books on the Internet at *www.compasspointbooks.com*
or e-mail your request to *custserv@compasspointbooks.com*

Photographs ©: Cover and p. 1: DigitalVision, p. 6: PhotoDisc/Ryan McVay, p. 7: Capstone
Press/Gary Sundermeyer, p. 7 background: PhotoDisc/Ryan McVay, p. 8: Capstone Press/Gary
Sundermeyer, p. 8 background: PhotoDisc/Ryan McVay, p. 9 bottom: Corbis/Dianna Sarto,
p. 9 top: Brand X Pictures/Photo 24, p. 10 bottom: Corbis, p. 10 top: Capstone Press/Gary
Sundermeyer, p. 11 bottom: Alan and Sandy Carey, p. 11 top: Creatas, p. 12 right:
DigitalVision, p. 12 left: Brand X Pictures/Guido Alberto Rossi

Editorial Development: Alice Dickstein, Alice Boynton
Photo Researcher: Wanda Winch
Design/Page Production: Silver Editions, Inc.

Library of Congress Cataloging-in-Publication Data
Cherrington, Janelle.
  Who needs teeth? / by Janelle Cherrington.
     p. cm. — (Compass Point phonics readers)
  Summary: Discusses human and animal teeth and what they do in
  easy-to-read text that incorporates phonics instruction and rebuses.
  Includes bibliographical references and index.
   ISBN 0-7565-0535-6 (hc)
   1. Teeth—Juvenile literature. 2. Reading—Phonetic method—Juvenile
  literature. [1. Teeth. 2. Rebuses. 3. Reading—Phonetic method.]
  I. Title. II. Series.
   QM311.C48 2003
   611'.314—dc21   2003006379

Table of Contents

Dear Parent or Caregiver,

Welcome to Compass Point Phonics Readers, books of information for young children. Each book concentrates on specific phonic sounds and words commonly found in beginning reading materials. Featuring eye-catching photographs, every book explores a single science or social studies concept that is sure to grab a child's interest.

So snuggle up with your child, and let's begin. Start by reading aloud the Mother Goose nursery rhyme on the next page. As you read, stress the words in dark type. These are the words that contain the phonic sounds featured in this book. After several readings, pause before the rhyming words, and let your child chime in.

Now let's read *Who Needs Teeth?* If your child is a beginning reader, have him or her first read it silently. Then ask your child to read it aloud. For children who are not yet reading, read the book aloud as you run your finger under the words. Ask your child to imitate, or "echo," what he or she has just heard.

Discussing the book's content with your child:
Explain that when children are babies, their first teeth grow in. Later, they lose those teeth, and new permanent teeth grow in.

At the back of the book is a fun Hop Scotch game. Your child will take pride in demonstrating his or her mastery of the phonic sounds and the high-frequency words.

Enjoy Compass Point Phonics Readers and watch your child read and learn!

Sleep, Baby, Sleep

Sleep, baby, **sleep,**
Father guards the **sheep;**
Mother shakes the **dreamland tree,**
And from it fall **sweet dreams** for **thee,**
Sleep, baby, **sleep.**

Sleep, baby **sleep,**
Our cottage vale is **deep;**
The little lamb is on the **green,**
With woolly **fleece** so soft and **clean—**
Sleep, baby, **sleep.**

Look in a  mirror and smile.
What do you see?
Teeth!
Why do we need teeth?

Teeth help us eat our food.
The woman bites into a big peach.
She uses her sharp teeth.
These teeth are made to bite.

She squashes and chews the peach.
She uses her side teeth.
Side teeth are wide and flat.
These teeth are made to chew.

These front teeth are small
and sharp.
They help the squirrel split
nuts and seeds.

These teeth are wide and flat.
They help the [horse] crush
grass and hay.

These teeth are long and sharp.
They help the [tiger] bite
and rip meat.

Which teeth can eat meat?
Which teeth can eat grass?

Word List

Long e (e, ea, ee)

e
she
the
we

ea
eat
meat
peach

ee
need(s)
see
seeds
teeth

r-, l-, and s-Blends

crush
grass
flat
smile
split
squashes

High-Frequency

long
why

Science

chew(s)
food
front
sharp

Hop Scotch

You will need:
- 1 penny
- 2 moving pieces, such as nickels or checkers

Player 1

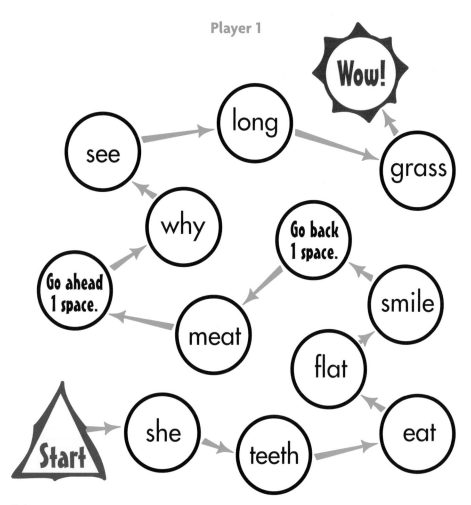

How to Play

- Each player puts a moving piece on his or her Start. Players take turns shaking the penny and dropping it on the table. Heads means move 1 space. Tails means move 2 spaces.
- The player moves and reads the word in the circle. If the child cannot read the word, tell him or her what it is. On the next turn, the child must read the word before moving.
- If a player lands on a circle having special directions, he or she should move accordingly.
- The first player to reach the *Wow!* sign wins the game.

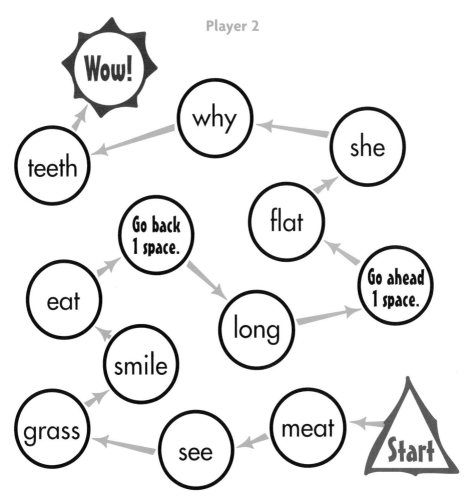

Player 2

Read More

Frost, Helen. *Brushing Well.* Mankato, Minn.: Pebble Books, 1999.

Frost, Helen. *Your Teeth.* Mankato, Minn.: Pebble Books, 1999.

Miles, Elizabeth. *Mouths and Teeth.* Animal Parts Series. Chicago, Ill.: Heinemann Library, 2003.

Schaefer, Lola M. *My Head.* It's My Body Series. Chicago, Ill.: Heinemann Library, 2003.

Index